NATURAL DISASTER Z⚡NE

HURRICANES AND TORNADOES

BEN HUBBARD

Cavendish
Square

Published in 2024 by Cavendish Square Publishing, LLC
2544 Clinton Street, Buffalo, NY 14224

Website: cavendishsq.com

Editor: Elise Short
Illustration and Design: Collaborate Agency

Picture Credits: All additional images courtesy of Shutterstock.

Cataloging-in-Publication Data

Names: Hubbard, Ben.
Title: Hurricanes and tornadoes / Ben Hubbard.
Description: Buffalo, New York: Cavendish Square Publishing, 2024. | Series: Natural disaster zone |
    Includes glossary and index
Identifiers: ISBN 9781502668288 (pbk) | ISBN 9781502668295 (library bound) |
    ISBN 9781502668301 (ebook)
Subjects: LCSH: Hurricanes-- Juvenile literature |Hurricane Mitch, 1998-- Juvenile literature | Natural
    Disasters--Juvenile literature | Storm Chasers--Juvenile literature | Tornadoes--Juvenile literature
Classification: LCC QC944.2 H83 2024 | DDC 551.55/2 --dc23

CPSIA compliance information: Batch #CSCSQ24: For further information contact Cavendish Square
Publishing LLC at 1-877-980-4450.

Printed in the United States of America

Find us on

CONTENTS

Introducing Tornadoes and Hurricanes   4
When a Tornado Strikes   6
What's in a Tornado?   8
Tornado Winds   10
CASE STUDY: Moore, 2013   12
Studying Tornadoes   14
Storm Chasers   16
When a Hurricane Hits   18
What Makes Hurricanes Form?   20
What's in a Hurricane?   22
Categories of Hurricane   24
CASE STUDY: Mitch, 1998   26
Studying Hurricanes   28

Glossary, Books, and Helpful Websites   30
Index   32

INTRODUCING TORNADOES AND HURRICANES

Tornadoes and hurricanes are super-charged storms that become deadly and destructive as they speed across land and sea. Both start as thunderstorms. Both are made up of violent, powerful winds that rotate around a peaceful central eye. However, their similarities end there.

WHAT ARE TORNADOES AND HURRICANES?

A tornado is a column of fast-moving, spinning air that can suck up a house and smash it into splinters.

A hurricane is a swirling mass of wind and clouds that feeds on warm seawater and unleashes gales and rain on land with monstrous force.

Tornadoes and hurricanes are among the most devastating natural disasters on Earth, and they have caused countless deaths and injuries.

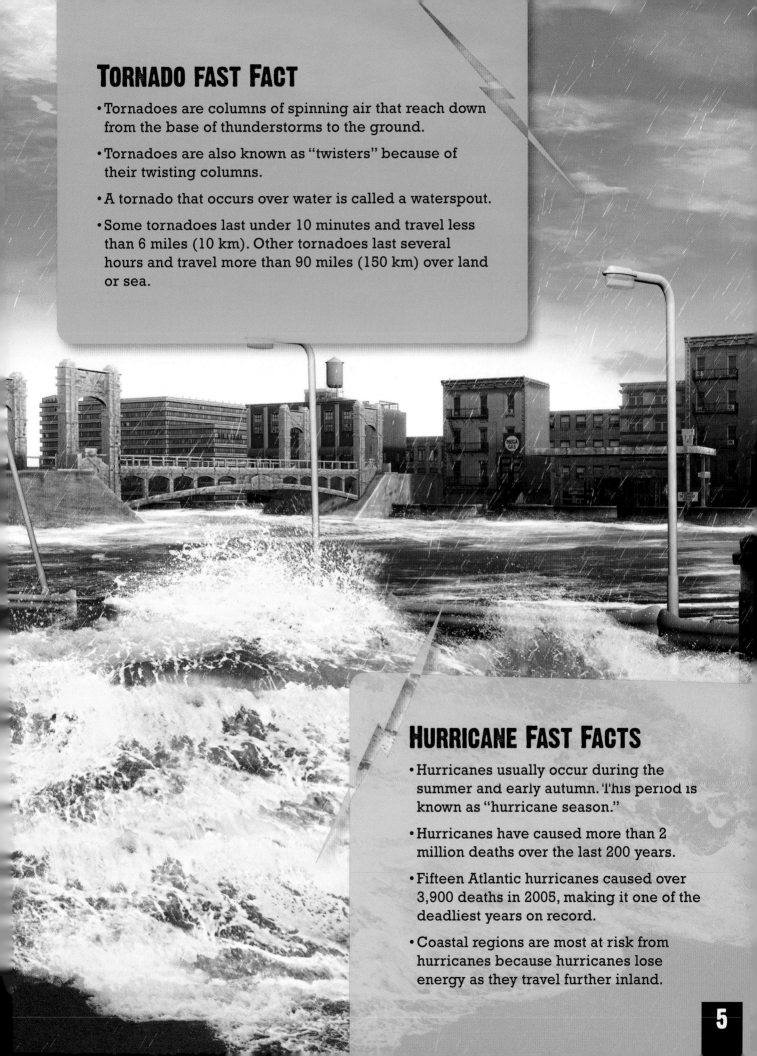

TORNADO FAST FACT

- Tornadoes are columns of spinning air that reach down from the base of thunderstorms to the ground.

- Tornadoes are also known as "twisters" because of their twisting columns.

- A tornado that occurs over water is called a waterspout.

- Some tornadoes last under 10 minutes and travel less than 6 miles (10 km). Other tornadoes last several hours and travel more than 90 miles (150 km) over land or sea.

HURRICANE FAST FACTS

- Hurricanes usually occur during the summer and early autumn. This period is known as "hurricane season."

- Hurricanes have caused more than 2 million deaths over the last 200 years.

- Fifteen Atlantic hurricanes caused over 3,900 deaths in 2005, making it one of the deadliest years on record.

- Coastal regions are most at risk from hurricanes because hurricanes lose energy as they travel further inland.

WHEN A TORNADO STRIKES

On April 26, 1989, the deadliest tornado on record struck the district of Manikganj, Bangladesh. At 6:30 pm, thick, black thunderclouds filled the sky, and the twisting end of a tornado was seen touching the ground. Quickly, the tornado grew to around 1 mile (1.5 km) wide. It then cut a 50-mile (80 km) path of devastation through one of Bangladesh's poorest regions.

DESTROYING DWELLINGS

The tornado reached wind speeds of 112-217 mph (180-350 kph) as it tore through the countryside. Within minutes, the tornado had uprooted every tree and destroyed every dwelling within a range of 2.3 square miles (6 sq km).

It continued its destruction as it blew through Manikganj and then obliterated the heavily-populated towns of Saturia and Daulatpur.

DROUGHTS AND DEVASTATION

The Daulatpur-Saturia tornado was part of a wider tornado outbreak that killed over 1,300 people and injured 12,000 more. It also made over 80,000 people instantly homeless and took away their livelihoods. This is because the tornadoes struck during a long drought in Bangladesh and many crops had completely dried out.

The dried-out crops were either blown away by the high speed winds or washed away by the heavy rains which followed. This led to famine and disease for the people of the area.

Faster Disaster Facts

- The high population density, poorly constructed buildings, and a lack of warning systems were held responsible for the high number of fatalities in the Daulatpur-Saturia tornado.

- The tornado caused more than US$900 million worth of damage.

- The Daulatpur-Saturia tornado was not the only tornado to claim lives in Bangladesh's Manikganj district. Another tornado in 1973 killed nearly 700 people.

Mountains and Thunderstorms

Tornadoes normally occur in Bangladesh from March to May, when cold, dry air from the Himalaya mountains encounters warm, wet air flowing in from the Bay of Bengal.

The Bangladesh thunderstorms that create tornadoes are also responsible for some of the world's largest and deadliest hailstones. During one 1986 thunderstorm, hailstones weighing up to 2 pounds (1 kg) killed 92 people in Bangladesh's Gopalganj district.

What's in a Tornado?

One of nature's most violent storms, a tornado is a fast-moving, rapidly-spinning column of air that twists down from a thunderstorm cloud. As it hits the ground, a tornado appears like a black funnel or a writhing piece of rope. A large tornado can snap tree trunks like matchsticks, flatten whole towns, and pick up trucks and toss them like toys.

Forming a Tornado

A tornado develops from a large thunderstorm cloud. A thunderstorm cloud is formed when warm, moist air rises from the ground and hits cool, dry air in the atmosphere. A rapidly rotating thunderstorm cloud creates the right conditions for a tornado to form.

The following stages illustrate how this happens.

2

A downdraft of cold air and water droplets pushes down from the cloud.

1

An updraft of warm air from the ground rises toward the thunderstorm cloud.

The Eye of the Storm

Although a tornado is made up of fast, destructive winds, its center—known as the eye—is calm and quiet. Some people who have been in the eye say it is like being in a huge pipe. Objects seen whirling around the eye have included clothes, cars, and cows.

3

Cross winds hitting the cloud from different directions cause it to rotate violently.

HEAD-SPINNING SIZES AND SPEEDS

A large tornado is a terrifying sight: It can grow to hundreds of feet wide, travel across land at over 60 mph (100 kph), and suck anything up in its path like a giant vacuum cleaner. Inside the largest tornadoes are winds spinning at over 300 mph (483 kph), making them sound like "1,000 freight trains," according to one eyewitness.

4

A funnel of rapidly rotating air forms and drops below the cloud, stretching towards the ground. When the funnel makes contact with the ground, it becomes a tornado.

5

Water droplets fall from the thunderstorm cloud into the tornado funnel, mixing with dust and debris rising from the ground. This gives the tornado its infamous black color.

TORNADO WINDS

The winds inside a tornado can reach 300 mph (483 kph) and suck up tons of soil, sand, or even asphalt from the road. Tornadoes can also pick up and fling massive objects. Trucks have been thrown down highways, refrigerators tossed hundreds of miles, and whole houses pushed down the road.

THE ENHANCED FUJITA SCALE

The strength of a tornado is based on its wind speeds. However, it is very difficult to measure the winds inside a tornado. Instead, the tornado's wind speeds are worked out from the damage that they cause. This is called the Enhanced Fujita (EF) Scale.

RATING EF2

WIND SPEED
111-135 mph
(178–217 kph)

DAMAGE
considerable damage: cars tossed, homes shifted, trees snapped

WIND SPEED

RATING EF1

WIND SPEED
86-110 mph
(138–177 kph)

DAMAGE
moderate damage: windows broken, roofs stripped

RATING EF0

WIND SPEED
65-85 mph
(104–137 kph)

DAMAGE
minor damage: branches broken off trees, parts of roofs blown off

RATING EF5

WIND SPEED
200+ mph
(322+ kph)

DAMAGE
incredible damage: trees snapped, houses swept away, high-rise buildings critically damaged

RATING EF3

WIND SPEED
136-165 mph
(218–266 kph)

DAMAGE
severe damage: large buildings damaged, trains overturned, trees debarked

RATING EF4

WIND SPEED
166-200 mph
(267–321 kph)

DAMAGE
extreme damage: houses leveled, trucks thrown significant distances

Odd Occurrences

Strange things can happen in the winds of a tornado. Once, a whole pond of frogs was sucked up and rained down on a nearby town. Another tornado lifted a stroller and baby high into the air and set it down unharmed several feet away. Tornadoes have also stripped people of their clothes, shorn sheep of their wool, and plucked feathers from a hen's back.

CASE STUDY: MOORE, USA, 2013

In May 2013, an outbreak of deadly tornadoes struck the state of Oklahoma. The outbreak lasted for over two weeks and included two rare EF5 tornadoes: the most powerful tornadoes on Earth. One of these tornadoes inflicted terrible damage as it carved a 14-mile (22-km) path of destruction through the heavily populated suburb of Moore.

CANADA

USA   Moore, Oklahoma

TORNADO TOUCHDOWN

On the morning of May 20, meteorologists at the National Weather Service (NWS) issued a tornado emergency for Moore.

With winds reaching 200 mph (320 kph), the tornado bulldozed its way through Moore. It reduced thousands of homes to rubble, destroyed two schools, and critically damaged a hospital.

The tornado only took 40 minutes to pass through the area, but it left a mountain of debris, crushed cars, and dead bodies in its wake.

THE HUMAN COST

Immediately after the tornado passed, firefighters, soldiers, and search and rescue teams began looking for survivors. Within 12 hours, 100 people had been dug out of the rubble.

Others, however, were not so lucky. The tornado had claimed 24 lives, including 10 children. Nearly 390 people had been badly injured, and 3,000 more had lost everything they owned in an instant. It later emerged that the schools and many homes did not have emergency storm shelters. This is despite Moore being one of the most tornado-prone areas in the region of the US known as "Tornado Alley."

TORNADO TOWN, USA

Moore has had quite an unlucky history with tornadoes. Of the nine EF5 tornadoes that have struck Oklahoma since 1950, two of them occurred in Moore! incredibly,

The path taken by the 2013 tornado was similar to another EF5 tornado that struck Moore in 1999 and an EF4 tornado that struck Moore in 2003. To make matters worse, 11 days after the Moore tornado, another EF5 tornado struck nearby El Reno and killed nine people.

Over 95 percent of all US tornadoes have an EF3 rating or below; in Tornado Alley, 25 percent of tornadoes are above EF3.

FASTER DISASTER FACTS

- When the tornado hit the nearby I-40 highway, it blew cars off the road, flipped over trucks, and demolished roadside buildings.

- Each search and rescue team working in Moore included 31 specialists, four sniffer dogs, and metal-cutting equipment.

- The cost of the damage to Moore caused by the tornado was over US$2 billion.

STUDYING TORNADOES

After a tornado has struck, scientists are often quick to visit the site. Tornado scientists are especially interested in examining the damage caused. This helps them estimate the tornado's strength so they can better understand it.

GATHERING EVIDENCE

Scientists visiting tornado zones are like policemen investigating a crime scene. First, they photograph and document the evidence, such as damage to buildings and how vehicles and other debris have been tossed around.

The scientists then examine the information against aerial satellite photos to see how the tornado behaved as it passed through. Finally, all of the scientists' data is fed into a "damage indicator" computer program to calculate the tornado's rating on the Enhanced Fujita Scale (see pages 10–11).

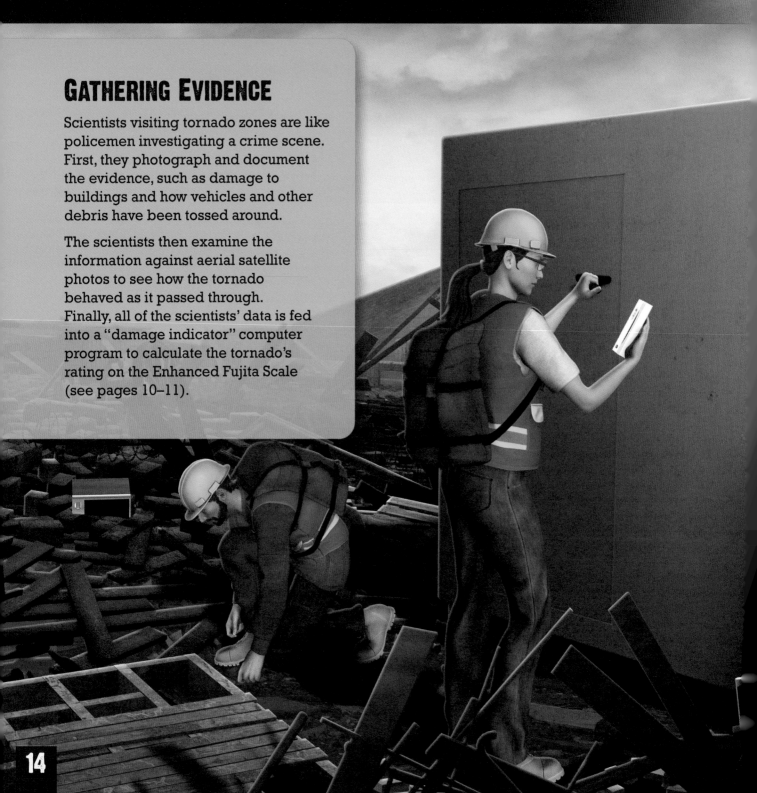

VORTEX2

The Verification of the Origins of Rotation in Tornadoes Experiment (VORTEX) was a series of scientific projects that ran from 1996 to 2010 and explored why some thunderstorms turn into tornadoes.

The projects employed over 100 scientists who used a fleet of vehicles to chase and study tornadoes. The scientists also used remote-controlled airplanes, weather balloons, and special probes that traveled into the center of a tornado to measure its winds.

STORM CENTERS

Not all tornado scientists visit tornado zones to study them. Some work in weather service centers trying to forecast tornadoes.

At the US National Weather Service's Storm Prediction Center, scientists closely monitor weather systems via satellite photographs and Doppler radar (see page 17).

Satellite photographs can show a swelling above a thundercloud, which is a telltale sign a tornado is about to form. Tornado alerts can then be issued to the public.

STORM CHASERS

Storm chasers are people who use specially-equipped vehicles to find and follow tornadoes. Some storm chasers are scientists studying how tornadoes behave. Others are professional meteorologists or television news cameramen. However, many storm chasers are amateurs wanting to become famous by taking videos and photos of violent tornadoes.

STORM CHASING VEHICLE

A storm chaser's vehicle is fitted with devices to find and record images of a freshly formed tornado. The typical equipment includes:

- digital cameras and webcams to record still and video images of a tornado

- laptop computer to monitor weather updates and radar and to upload images from cameras

- cell phone to connect the laptop to the internet via Bluetooth

- citizens band (CB) radio to talk to other storm chasers

- global positioning system (GPS) unit to find tornado locations given by other storm chasers

DOPPLER ON WHEELS

A Doppler radar is a special forecasting tool that can measure the location, direction, and wind speed of a thunderstorm. This means a Doppler is the first to predict when a thunderstorm is about to become a tornado. Mobile Doppler vehicles are used widely in Tornado Alley.

HELP OR HINDRANCE?

Storm chasers send vital information about tornadoes to meteorological offices so the public can be warned. However, some say the large number of amateur storm chasers makes the occupation dangerous. This is because amateur storm chasers are often inexperienced and ill-equipped, and they block the way of professional storm chasers trying to get through.

WHEN A HURRICANE HITS

On August 23, 2005, a storm known as a tropical depression formed over the Bahamas in the Atlantic Ocean. For two days, the storm gathered strength before making landfall on the Florida coast. This hurricane was given the name Katrina. It became one of deadliest and costliest natural disasters in US history.

USA

New Orleans

Hurricane
Katrina's
path

MEXICO

Gulf of
Mexico

STRIKING NEW ORLEANS

Hurricane Katrina struck New Orleans with devastating winds, torrential rainfall, and a 30-foot (9 m) wall of water known as a storm surge (see page 23).

By August 30, 80 percent of the city was underwater. This triggered a massive displacement of people and a humanitarian crisis.

By September 1, food and water shortages had begun and the bacteria in the floodwaters caused a public health emergency. Katrina had caused 1,833 deaths, over US$108 billion in damages, and the destruction of hundreds of thousands of homes.

SUCKING UP SEAWATER

Katrina spent five hours over Florida before crossing into the Gulf of Mexico. Here, the hurricane sucked up the gulf's warm waters and strengthened to become a Category 4 hurricane.

On August 29, Katrina struck the US's south coast with devastating winds reaching 170 mph (275 kph). Katrina destroyed homes and power lines in the states of Mississippi, Alabama ,and Louisiana. However, the worst damage occurred when the hurricane reached the city of New Orleans in Louisiana. Here, 100,000 people remained in the city, while 1 million more had followed the evacuation order and fled.

FASTER DISASTER FACTS

- It is thought that Katrina became a Category 5 hurricane over the Gulf of Mexico but turned into a Category 4 as it made landfall.

- Hurricane relief shelters housed 273,000 people at the peak of the disaster.

- Following the disaster, people from 114,000 households had to be housed in trailers.

- The impact of Katrina was felt over an 89,962-square-mile (233,000 sq km) area of the southern United States.

NEW ORLEANS UNDER WATER

During Hurricane Katrina, around 40 percent of the deaths in Louisiana were caused by drowning. This was due to the extensive flooding in New Orleans mainly caused by the city's levees (river banks) and flood walls breaking under the strain of the hurricane. Some areas were 10 feet (3 m) underwater.

New Orleans stayed flooded for 43 days after Katrina, until all of the floodwater could be pumped out. Over 70 percent of the houses in New Orleans were damaged by the hurricane and the subsequent flooding.

WHAT MAKES HURRICANES FORM?

Hurricanes are like giant heat engines that use warm, moist air as fuel. This is why they form over tropical oceans where the water has a temperature of at least 80°F (27°C). When this warm moisture is sucked up and and combined with wind, a hurricane is born.

A hurricane often begins its life as a simple thunderstorm. Conditions have to be exactly right for it to become a hurricane. **This is how it happens:**

STAGE 1: TROPICAL DISTURBANCE

A hurricane begins as a tropical disturbance. This is formed when seawater evaporates into water vapor and rises upward to become storm clouds. The storm clouds form columns around 10.5 miles (17 km) above sea level. Air is also sucked in from below the clouds to join the columns.

STAGE 2: TROPICAL DEPRESSION

As more air rises into the cloud columns, wind is created. This wind spins in a circular motion, which is caused by the Earth's rotation. The clouds and wind begin to whip around a central point at a speed of up to 38 mph (61 kph). This is called a tropical depression.

STAGE 3:
TROPICAL STORM

If the tropical depression's wind speeds exceed 38 mph (61 kph), it becomes a tropical storm. The fast winds now twist and turn around the center of the storm, known as its eye. In the northern hemisphere, the wind turns counterclockwise. In the southern hemisphere, it turns clockwise. This is known as the Coriolis effect.

STAGE 4:
HURRICANE

When the wind speeds reach 75 mph (120 kph), a tropical storm officially becomes a hurricane. At this stage, the storm clouds are usually around 9.5 miles (15 km) high and around 124 miles (200 km) across. The eye is between 5 and 17 miles (8 and 28 km) wide. As it travels over the water, the hurricane gets stronger and deadlier until it reaches land.

WHAT'S IN A HURRICANE?

A large hurricane contains wind speeds of over 160 mph (257 kph) and can unleash more than 2.3 trillion gallons (9 trillion liters) of rain per day.

ANATOMY OF A HURRICANE

The main two ingredients needed for a hurricane are wind and warm water. Together, these combine inside a hurricane to create a perfect storm. **Below are the different parts of a hurricane.**

Dry air descends down through the eye toward the bottom.

Warm, moist air rushes in toward the center of the hurricane, called its eye.

The hurricane travels as it rotates.

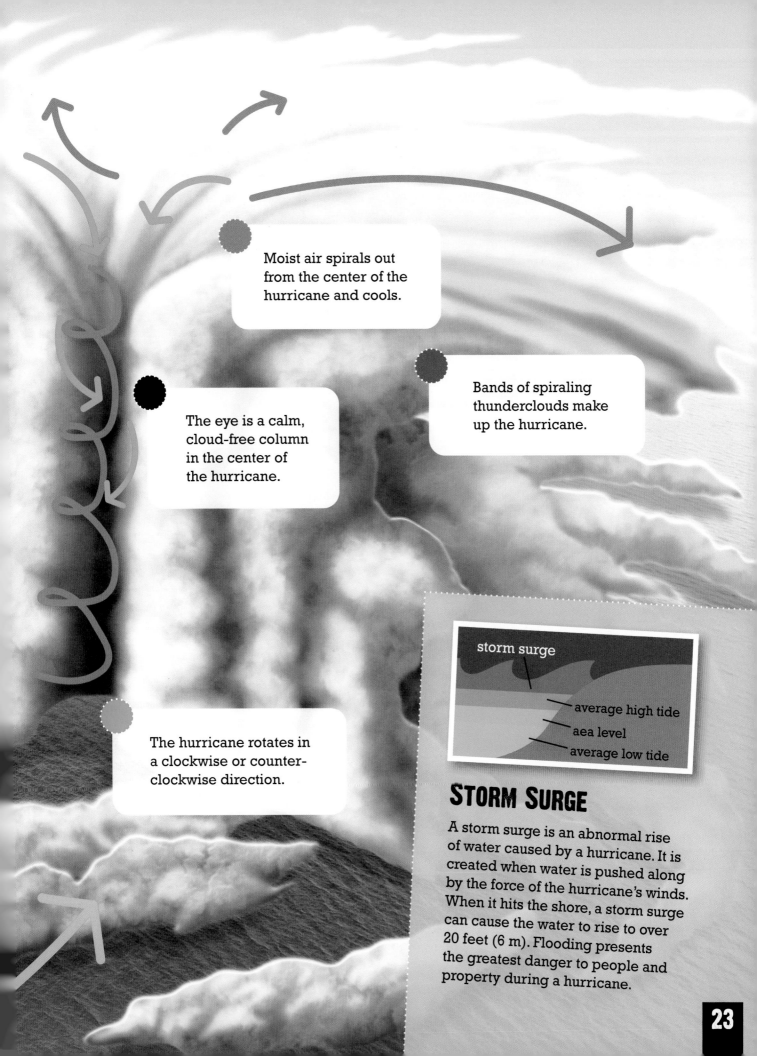

Moist air spirals out from the center of the hurricane and cools.

Bands of spiraling thunderclouds make up the hurricane.

The eye is a calm, cloud-free column in the center of the hurricane.

The hurricane rotates in a clockwise or counter-clockwise direction.

storm surge

average high tide

aea level

average low tide

STORM SURGE

A storm surge is an abnormal rise of water caused by a hurricane. It is created when water is pushed along by the force of the hurricane's winds. When it hits the shore, a storm surge can cause the water to rise to over 20 feet (6 m). Flooding presents the greatest danger to people and property during a hurricane.

CATEGORIES OF HURRICANE

Not all hurricanes have the same deadly power. Some suck up warm seawater and wind and wreak destruction on coastlines and islands. Others change course or fizzle out before they reach the shore. Once on land, a hurricane dies out because it no longer has warm water to fuel it. Before then, a hurricane is rated and given a category of 1 to 5.

HURRICANE CATEGORIES

The Saffir-Simpson Hurricane Wind Scale gives a hurricane a 1–5 rating based on its wind speed and the damage it causes. **The different categories are shown below.**

Atlantic Ocean

Pacific Ocean

CATEGORY 3:
WINDS OF 111-129 MPH (178—208 KPH)

Devastating damage will occur. Houses will sustain major damage to roofs. Many trees will be snapped or uprooted and block numerous roads.

CATEGORY 2:
WINDS OF 96-110 MPH (154—177 KPH)

Extremely dangerous winds will damage house roofs and walls. Small trees will be uprooted and block roads. Power lines may be out for many weeks.

CATEGORY 1:
WINDS OF 74-95 MPH (119–153 KPH)

Very dangerous winds will produce some damage to homes. Large tree branches will snap and power lines may be brought down.

CATEGORY 4:
WINDS OF 130-156 MPH
(209—251 KPH)

Catastrophic damage will occur. Houses will lose their roofs and some exterior walls. Most trees and power lines will be snapped or uprooted. There will be no power supply for weeks or months.

CATEGORY 5:
WINDS OF 157+ MPH
(252 KPH+)

Utterly catastrophic damage will occur. Most houses will be destroyed. Fallen trees and power lines will block access to residential areas. Power will be out for many months. Most of the area will be uninhabitable for months or years.

Indian Ocean

Pacific Ocean

HURRICANE AREAS

This map shows the areas (in pink) where hurricanes are most likely to occur around the world. Hurricanes are called different names in different countries, but they are all the same type of storm. In the Atlantic Ocean, the storms are called hurricanes; in the Indian Ocean, cyclones; and in the Pacific Ocean, typhoons.

CASE STUDY: MITCH, 1998

In 1998, an extremely hot summer struck the Caribbean. Sea temperatures reached 80°F (27°C), and in October, a tropical depression formed. By October 25, the depression had turned into a Category 5 hurricane named Mitch. As its winds reached 180 mph (290 kph), with gusts of 200 mph (321 kph), Mitch made landfall in the country of Honduras.

FLOODS AND MUDSLIDES

Mitch caused widespread devastation and loss of life as it struck Central America. Honduras and Nicaragua were the worst affected. The heavy rainfall caused floods and mudslides, which destroyed crop fields and washed away entire villages.

Roads and bridges were destroyed, making it difficult for emergency crews to reach people in need.

THE HUMAN COST

Hurricane Mitch left terrible damage in its wake as it passed through Central America and weakened into a tropical storm. Hundreds of thousands of homes had been obliterated in Honduras and Nicaragua, with parts of Guatemala, Belize, and El Salvador also affected.

Over 11,000 people had been killed in the hurricane, 11,000 more were missing, and 2.7 million were left homeless. It was the second-deadliest Atlantic hurricane on record. The deadliest was called the Great Hurricane of 1780.

A Very Intense Hurricane

After it made landfall, Mitch's winds dropped from 180 mph (290 kph) to 80 mph (130 kph). This did not stop it from releasing a record rainfall of 4 inches (100 mm) per hour on Honduras, Guatemala, and Nicaragua. The total rainfall was 50 inches (1,250 mm).

Mitch was ranked 8th on the chart of most intense Atlantic hurricanes. Following the disaster, Mitch was forever taken off the list of hurricane names. The new M-name was Matthew.

The remnants of Mitch reached the UK 15 days after it had become a hurricane in the Caribbean.

Faster Disaster Facts

• Polluted drinking water caused by the floodwaters led to outbreaks of disease, including cholera.

• Over 2,000 people died in one mudslide in Posoltega, Nicaragua.

• Mexico and the US sent supplies, helicopters, and troops to help search for survivors in the rubble.

• Massive rebuilding had to take place in Honduras and Nicaragua, including new schools, hospitals, and roads. Farmland also had to be replanted.

• Hurricane Mitch is estimated to have caused over US$6 million in damages.

STUDYING HURRICANES

By studying hurricanes, scientists hope to predict their behavior and prevent loss of life. However, hurricanes are difficult to study. They can quickly change course or destroy scientific equipment and kill the people using it. Studying hurricanes is a dangerous business.

HURRICANE HUNTERS

The best way to accurately study a hurricane is to get inside it. To do this, scientists fly specially built "hurricane hunter" planes into the storm's "eyewall." The eyewall is the ring of thunderclouds that surrounds the hurricane's eye. Here, the scientists use sensors to measure the hurricane's size and structure before sending the information back to the hurricane center or meteorological office.

Small instruments called "dropsondes" are also dropped from the plane to record information about the hurricane's temperature, wind speed, and humidity. As the dropsondes parachute down, they send the data to the hurricane center via satellite.

HURRICANE CENTER

Hurricane centers are where scientists and meteorologists keep a watch out for developing hurricanes. Using data sent from satellites and hurricane hunter planes, hurricane centers issue forecasts and weather warnings to areas that sit in a hurricane's path.

However, hurricanes are extremely unpredictable: They can easily change course and strike unexpectedly elsewhere. No one can be completely sure what a hurricane is going to do next.

SATELLITE REPORTS

Satellites in space take photos of storms as they develop and grow. Other satellites have sensors that record the temperature of the ocean's surface seawater. This data is beamed back to hurricane centers, where it is used to try to predict whether a storm will develop into a hurricane. It is from satellite pictures that people on Earth are able to see the white, donut-shaped eyewall of clouds that surround a hurricane's eye.

HURRICANE NAMES

If a hurricane's winds are recorded at 38.5 mph (62 kph) or above, then it is officially named. Names go in alphabetical order and are drawn up from a list six years in advance. The names of the most devastating hurricanes, such as Andrew, are withdrawn from the list and not used again.

GLOSSARY, BOOKS, AND HELPFUL WEBSITES

GLOSSARY

amateur
Someone—in this case, a storm chaser—who is not paid, as opposed to a professional who does the same job for money.

asphalt
A black material used to pave roads.

bacteria
Microorganisms—some of which can cause disease—living in and around humans.

Bluetooth
A way of wirelessly connecting to cell phones, computers, and other electronic devices.

casualty
Someone who is dead or injured as a result of an accident, a war, or an incident.

catastrophe
A disastrous event that causes great damage and suffering.

cholera
A serious disease caught from dirty drinking water that causes vomiting and diarrhea.

debris
Pieces of garbage and the remains of buildings that are scattered everywhere.

diameter
The length of a straight line that runs through the center of an object or space.

drought
A long period with little or no rain.

downdraft
An air current that flows downward.

Doppler radar
A radar tracking system used to determine the location and speed of a storm, clouds, precipitation, etc.

dwelling
A shelter, such as a house, where people live.

equator
The imaginary line drawn on Earth halfway between the North and South poles.

evacuation
The orderly removal of people from a place to avoid a disaster.

evaporate
To cause a liquid to change to a gas, especially by heating.

famine
A great lack of food over a wide area.

humanitarian crisis
An event that causes widespread human suffering.

landfall
Arrival at land from the sea or air.

livelihood
The means of supporting oneself, such as a job.

meteorology
The study of the science of weather.

northern hemisphere
The half of the Earth that is above the equator.

rubble
Broken fragments of rock and brick left behind after the destruction of a building.

satellite
An object that orbits a star or planet. Many Earth satellites are manmade objects that can take photos and record data about the planet.

southern hemisphere
The half of the Earth that is below the equator.

torrential
A great outpouring.

updraft
An air current that flows upward.

BOOKS

Devastating Storms (Mother Nature Is Trying to Kill Me!) by Janey Levy (Gareth Stevens, 2020)

Hurricanes (Nature Unleashed) by Louise and Richard Spilsbury (Franklin Watts, 2018)

Hurricanes and Tornadoes (Transforming Earth's Geography) by Joanna Brundle (KidHaven, 2018)

Our Planet Earth (Cause, Effect and Chaos!) by Paul Mason (Wayland, 2018)

HELPFUL WEBSITES

These websites for kids are all about tornadoes and hurricanes:

www.natgeokids.com/uk/discover/geography/physical-geography/tornado-facts/

www.weatherwizkids.com/weather-tornado.htm

www.natgeokids.com/uk/discover/geography/physical-geography/hurricanes/

www.esa.int/esaKIDSen/SEMCH4YDE2E_Earth_0.html

INDEX

B
Bangladesh 6–7

C
Central America 26–27
centers, hurricane 28–29
chasers, storm 15–17
Coriolis effect 21
cyclones, tropical 25

D
Daulatpur-Saturia tornado
    6–7
depression, tropical 18,
    20–21, 26
disturbance, tropical 20
dropsondes 28

E
Enhanced Fujita Scale (EF)
    10–11, 14
eye (of a tornado/
    hurricane) 4, 8, 21–22, 28
eyewalls 28–29

F
flooding 18–19, 23, 26–27

H
hailstones 7
hunters, hurricane 28–29
Hurricane Katrina, US
    18–19
Hurricane Mitch,
    Caribbean 26–27
hurricane season 5
hurricanes 4–5, 18–29
    categories 24–26
    how they form 20–23

M
meteorological offices 15,
    17, 28
meteorologists 12–17, 28
Moore tornadoes, US 12–13
mudslides 26–27

N
National Weather Service,
    US 12–13, 15, 17
New Orleans 18–19

R
radar, Doppler 15, 17

S
Saffir-Simpson Hurricane
    Wind Scale 24–25
satellites 14–15, 28–29
scientists, tornado/
    hurricane 14–16, 28–29
shelters, hurricane 19
storm, tropical 21, 26
surge, storm 18, 23

T
Tornado Alley 12–13, 17
tornadoes 4–17
    how they form 8–9
    wind speeds 10–11
twisters 5
typhoons 25

U
USA 12–13, 17–19, 26–27

V
VORTEX 15

W
waterspouts 5